Dreams of Passing Fire

Dreams of Passing Fire

Companion Poems from the Camino

Katherine January
Rebecca Ring

SHANTI ARTS PUBLISHING
BRUNSWICK, MAINE

Dreams of Passing Fire: Companion Poems from the Camino

Copyright © 2024 Katherine January and Rebecca Ring
All Rights Reserved

No part of this document may be reproduced or transmitted in any form or by any means without prior written permission of the publisher, except where permitted by law.

Published by Shanti Arts Publishing

Designed by Shanti Arts Designs

All photographs by the authors and used with their permission

Shanti Arts LLC
193 Hillside Road
Brunswick, Maine 04011
shantiarts.com

Printed in the United States of America

ISBN: 978-1-962082-31-0 (softcover)

Library of Congress Control Number: 2024941461

for those who've walked on without us

Contents

Acknowledgments / 9
Introduction / 11

I
In Our Veins / 17
A Dream of Passing Fire / 19

II
Walking My Way through Divorce / 25
To Estella / 27
Packing for the Camino / 32
three point seven ounces / 35

III
Before Birds / 40
Starting in the Dark / 42
The Red Kite / 46
Curve / 48
Rounding the Corner / 50

IV
Tandem / 54
All the Marys / 56
Tended by Bells / 58
Belorado / 60
The Olive Grove / 63
What I Didn't Know / 65

V
Laundry on the Camino / 70
Ablutions / 74
The Man in the White Linen Suit / 76
Alchemy / 78
Rogue in the House
    of Santo Domingo / 82
Unwitnessed / 84

VI
Rearview / 89
Entering Burgos / 91
Clouds over Burgos / 95

VII
Making Room / 100
Seeds / 102
Love Letter to a Poet / 106
The Knowing that Comes
    from Walking Through / 108

About the Authors / 111

Acknowledgments

We wish to express gratitude to—

Katherine's family: Craig, Maggie, Seth, and Durga, whose support is unwavering, who listen to her poems and want more, who help her see worlds she would otherwise miss, who make her happy to come home to hearth and garden after trekking somewhere far away;

Rebecca's family: Michel, Bianca, Olivia, and Tibeau, for saying yes to her escapades, whether she's on a trail in Spain or tethered to her computer, who form the rock on which she stands and enrich her life with laughter, insight, love, and joy, and her parents, who have supported her writing since childhood, even when it took her down a different path from theirs;

Christine Cote and Shanti Arts, for grasping the vision of this book, bringing it to reality, and for being a delight to work with;

the editor of *Last Stanza Poetry Journal* in which "Starting in the Dark" first appeared;

our manuscript readers, Annette Weed, Chris Chambers, Karen Concannon, and Maggie Milligan, who believed in what we were doing and made invaluable suggestions;

members of the Offweek Writers writing group, for listening to early drafts and always being eager to hear next installments;

Pam and Willy Littig, for believing we could walk that far, for sending us off to the Camino with good advice, encouragement, and lightweight water bottles;

—continued

the Salt Lake Chapter of American Pilgrims on the Camino, for gracing us with a Shell Ceremony when we departed and listening to our stories when we returned;

albergue hosts, for their hospitality and generosity of spirit;

other walkers and people we met along the Camino, for the mystery and pleasure of a chance encounter when their passage intersected with ours;

the landscape of Spain—sunflowers, olives, calendula, grapes—for offering unconditional beauty and surprise no matter the weather, no matter the season, no matter our ability to see it; and

each other, for being trustworthy companions who—in walking and in writing—encouraged and pulled the best out of each other and who embraced the vision of this book and the shoulder-to-shoulder process of making it happen.

Introduction

We knew each other as writers, not as walkers, and not in the way we would come to. Together, we set out in September of 2019 to traverse what we could of an ancient path across the whole of northern Spain. Trod for hundreds of years, the Camino de Santiago is still traveled by modern pilgrims seeking to disconnect from the everyday and explore new landscapes both inner and earthly.

As we walked, we discovered that the journey was not only about disconnecting and going inward, but also about connecting—conversation beginning in the shadow of a town and ending in an olive grove, crusty bread passed hand to hand by travelers of all ages and origins, tired feet soaking in a basin at the end of the day. We found in those we met—and in each other—the shared experience of seekers.

With every step, the two of us became better friends. We followed the same trail but allowed each other the silence and separateness of our inner journeys. We snatched moments to journal, but our focus was on the path in front of us, not on writing. We certainly never envisioned a collection of companion poems.

After walking 200 miles through towns and forests and vineyards, we agreed to return the following year to finish the remaining 284 miles. But that never happened. Less than six months later, the world went into lockdown, and a pandemic erased overnight the possibility of another Camino trek. Sharing pilgrim meals around long tables and sleeping in *albergues* (hostels) in close proximity with strangers became not only impossible but unthinkable. Still we held out hope that it would pass and we would soon be back on the trail. By summer, it became clear we would not. We would not be flying to Spain in the fall to complete the Camino.

—continued

So we decided to travel a different way.

As we had on foot, we walked the path of our Camino experience, but this time in words. We began from a common starting place—a town, an image, an encounter—then dove inward. Writing instead of walking. Journeying the path together, but separately. In steps. In poems. In tandem.

—KCJ & RR

I

In Our Veins

We woke, in those days, before the sun
to whispers and the slide of bedding
zips and clicks
the cadences of women
stalking the tail of night. Both of us
peering into the dark
that with every footstep grew lighter
until our shadows
loomed across fields of dry
and sentinel September
sunflowers. You,
transfixed
by wizened faces marching
across the dawn expanse.
So many miles ahead of us
and there, in the palm of each hill
a refuge.

—continued

It is the refuge of friendship
sheltering us now
the shared memory of weight
on our backs, water in our mouths,
blisters in our socks and still
joy in our step.

Now we carry olive
grove and fig tree, travelers
passed and greeted, the sweet
juice of the *Rioja*
in our veins, almonds
in our pockets, remembrance
of embrace and smile, togetherness
of strangers, of us

light as wind
under the wings of a kite.

—*RR*

A Dream of Passing Fire

The first night, before we crossed
the Pyrenees on the French side
I dreamed I was passing fire to others
as we crouched in the shadow
of a huge red rock

We were all there, and we were passing
fire. Bowls of fire. In clay pots.
Nothing could be seen but the flicker
of light on rock

This was not a relic of Atapuerca
where fragments of ancient humans
had been found among stones.
This was different

This was the way it feels to be alone—yet not be

—continued

This was a small stringed song
in a courtyard at dusk. Chorizo
and fried egg on warm bread.
An open-sided barn, a man and his son
sorting almonds in an old tin tub.
Fresh figs, hidden
until someone showed us
how to look behind the leaves.
Grapes full to bursting
and legions of sunflowers past flowering
heavy brown heads
bowing together
dying together

no gold left in their faces
but when we looked

all we saw was gold

—*KCJ*

II

Walking My Way through Divorce

even now I find bits of his nylon cord
carefully bundled all over the house
white, black, red, green
coiled and tucked in drawers and cupboards
as if knots could make a difference
like they did that time in Wakeeney, Kansas
when the tent held fast in a storm

all those knots—tied, untied, never tied
could only do so much—he lost interest in knots
and I didn't know a slip knot from a sheep shank

but one day, without ever having been an Eagle Scout
I tucked a bundle of that cord into my Camino-bound pack
where the motion of daily walking on a pilgrim path
made more sense than anything

and when clouds were heavy
boots were heavy
hope for sleep was scarce
the bright red of that sturdy line whispered, *improvise*

hang your sodden clothes
above rows of narrow cots, mend a broken lace
on a boot, tie a tarp to a tree
when you are late and the hostels are full

—continued

right knot or wrong knot, cord in a cupboard
means memories, but cord in a boot means motion

town to town
vineyard to vineyard
sun to moon to milky way

walking set us free—all of us who trekked west
for reasons known, unknown and still emerging
the mud and mire of a late day storm
might sap our fragile resolve
but in the peach and purple dawn
we laced up boots and walked again

the motion reminding us to live
not outside this day
but in it, not in fear of the storm
but in it

all the way to the end
and then, one day more

—KCJ

To Estella

Children's voices behind us
made us turn and yield the path.
Backpacks loose upon their shoulders
their chattering and clucking
bounced off the vineyard, echoed
against the hill, dared the sunflowers
to turn their way, pay attention.
A parade of them
only two or three adults, only one
thing that could be, a school group.

Twenty years of fourteen
field trips each, the sounds
of nine and ten-year-olds
still ringing in my ears, I recognized
the elation unleashed
the vigilance of their teachers
the joyous clatter. Yes,
I thought, yes, I know the joy
of their liberation. I walk now
in celebration of mine.

—continued

I had run to the world
open-armed on the day of my retirement
when good-bye was bittersweet
the days ahead outnumbered by the ones behind
when my winnings—the flare of insight
in a pair of young eyes—
fell short in the weighing.
I'd clapped the dust from the erasers
never thinking
to encounter it down the road.

Then one of the young teachers
drew us into conversation.
A field trip, she told us in English,
to Estella
a town we'd planned to pass through.

Look, I imagined her saying, *a perfect example
of Homo peregrinas americanus. See how they walk
despite the ache in their knees
the weight and burdens they carry. They
follow the yellow arrows, The Way. And you
too, will have burdens of your own one day.*

Of course, I thought, shouldn't
every Spanish schoolchild be taught
to carry a pack, *walk the Camino?*
My students had learned about earthquakes
and pioneers, visited mountain ranges, wetlands
and salty lakes—but not
the Camino de Santiago.

That was something I'd had to fly
to Spain for, give myself
permission for, distance myself
from those twenty years for.

What we
at our age and in our foreignness
had embarked upon
looked so effortless on their backs
an escape from the classroom
a chance to tell tales out of earshot
—and for one boy, a way
to strut his command of English
to communicate what truly mattered.

—continued

He broke
from his clutch of friends, took a few steps
off the path to shout at me

"Minecraft!"

a video game any of my fourth graders
would've had on their mind. But he didn't
expect the smile
and the echo
from me

"Minecraft!"

I had wanted Estella to mean
star, something to reach for
but it's only a name, a town
we would pass by. And
on our way

the light in his face
the startle of his sudden win
and mine.

—RR

Packing for the Camino

we read blogs, talked to seasoned walkers, but in the end, it came down
to ounces, and how could we know what would matter

how could we know the headlamps we bought were not for walking
in the dark (there was moon for that, and the feel of dirt underfoot)

that headlamps were for rising, stealthy, fumbling for pants and socks
so as not to wake the others with an overhead bulb

that one ounce of almonds was the sacred cache of strength
that would see us through to potatoes, onions, and eggs five miles away

that chocolate was not optional, that paired with water
and the bread secured to our packs, footfall would be lighter

socks, yes, but how could we know those short ones from Vermont
with the mountain outline would be the toughest, dry the fastest

how could we know Compeed would cushion our blisters for days
when Moleskin or Band-Aids wouldn't last the afternoon

we took a chance on soap, but for fewer ounces, CampSuds washed body
clothes *and* hair, the late afternoon sun finishing what a tiny towel began

wind would have made a sail out of the ponchos we didn't take, jackets
kept us dry enough, and we walked off what dripped down the edges

as writers we couldn't leave paper behind, the thin-skinned journal
catching our tumbled words before bed (I had imagined moments

in a hayfield or a vineyard, poems caught on the fly) but walking
took what we had and left scraps for words at the end of the day

how could we know some fountains would give wine, some water, that
water in a basin could soak away doubt, as well as the ache in our feet

in the end, it wasn't what we carried or left behind that pulled
our arms *happy! happy!* to the sky, it was what we found by the side

of the road, the unexpected mirth in Logrono of people dressed
up for a wedding, the warm almond cookie early one Sunday

in Pamplona, where men with brooms were rinsing clean
the streets bulls had charged only weeks before, it was you

grinning, and holding your hiking poles as if they were horns, you
the stampeding bull, and nothing could be done to stop you

—*KCJ*

three point seven ounces

doesn't sound like much
the weight of a dream
or a sunbeam, but the numbers
weren't adding up

I'd never wanted a kitchen scale
        never found a reason
to weigh ingredients
        but now a need
to weigh belongings
        as if something crucial
        depended on the math

ten percent of your body weight

hard to measure against comfort
and habit
until you try to stuff that number
and no more
into something you can carry
on your back
for hundreds of miles
could I
afford this coat and really
how many shirts
does one need? In the end

—continued

the one thing
        that weighed what it weighed
        and no amount of math could render useless
was small, an essential
three point seven ounces (a bit more
with the breath I'd blow in at night
the extra load gone by morning)

and night after night
        when sleep would not come
        and then did and then didn't
        and then did again
it earned its weight
and the weight it carried

so
each morning

I folded and stuffed
that blessed thing
into its tiny sack, then into its niche
praised the dreams that pillow
had borne, the neck
it had cradled still able
to heft a pack that might have grown
heavier each day if not
for the slumber that came
on its airy loft, enough

for another day

—RR

III

Before Birds

the first rustle does not awaken
but the gradual
breaching of arms and legs
delivers a realization
I am late for something
no one told me about

we rise before dawn
moving like burglars
in some sleeping strangers' house
to discover the sleepers
have risen and departed

streetlights
on cobblestone, a blackened
sky and clotted sheep
around the moon
we take our first steps
into the dark, breath
slow and regular
like dreamers who've stayed
abed, voiceless supplicants
of the dawn watching for an open
café, or will we walk on, get a head
start and think later
of *¿café con leche?*

as the mist
about us turns ever paler
indigo, the road ahead
obscured, the steps of foot travelers
passing, all of us
sleepwalk toward the next
village, but so quiet

like morning fog
haunting each golden
belltower, each stride
taking us closer
to day

I am fever alert
a stringed instrument
ripe
to be plucked
wordless
on the road before birds

silent
so foggy silent, so dark
in the lightening
of morning

    —RR

Starting in the Dark

just last night the plaza brimmed
with wedding guests spilling from an uphill church
and pilgrims like us seeking wine and almond cake
but all is empty by the time
we unlatch the door of our *albergue*
in the still-dark early day

a single glass abandoned on a table
catches light from a street lamp
but the lamps run out at the end of town
and we go it alone, the moon
clawing its way through spools
and spools of unruly night cotton
left over from the storm

fog gobbles what little light there is
and, not quite awake, we float
like ghosts through milky mist
one slow step at a time
on a path we can't quite see

we want yellow
day yellow
sunflower yellow

we want a church
tall on a hill in the next town

we want coffee
we want bread
we want the path
firm beneath our feet
but morning is slow to brighten, and in our plodding way
we take what is in front of us to take

the crunch of almonds forgotten in our packs
the smell of centuries of seekers
the wet wood of waking trees

the surprise of a tiny hive-shaped house
in a stone-strewn field, the monk
who must have lived here, the doves he fed

tiny snails clinging to weeds like the spit of a spider
fleetingly azure in the half-light of dawn

we had started in the dark so we wouldn't miss this

and after fog
after night
after shadows scuttle deep into forest
we stop   we rest   we watch
while birds, white
black
black and white
wheel high in the now blue sky

—KCJ

The Red Kite

finds her sweet spot hanging mid-air
high above the Pyrenees
high above the Camino
a raptor once rare going nowhere

she could let the wind take her
but today, with a slight shift of wing
she makes a nest of the air
flapping just enough to fly in place

her wings as powerful now
as when they slice
the air on a hunt
or dive through rough trees

powerful enough to cradle her
in her chosen place
high above the sheep and wheat
and low-hung mist

and when her wings decide to go
they will remember everything
they need to know
about flight

everything they need to know
about finding the next valley
the next steel-sculpted cloud
the next mountain
wet and dangerous with almost-snow

the language of wind indecipherable
except to her, elusive as the yellow arrow
which points to Roncevalles

but can't spell out the way

—KCJ

Curve Around another bend in the road waits
the unknown. Every time. This one's swell
of squat, crumbling wall betrays a house
medieval, warped, and vacant under
layers of black and red clay tile
naked in its years of repair
disrepair. Inoccupancy.
Yet even now an iron
rooster crows
from atop
the roof
to say
the wind
still blows
this way. I am
only a traveler who
seeks the feral guidance
of an unencumbered wind.
So I stop for a breathless moment
to suck in the fullish scent of moss, clay
diesel, asphalt—and something older, urgent
impelling me on, to the next curve in the road.

—*RR*

Rounding the Corner

ancient tile troughed in moss, red on gray
on green, doorways more whittled than milled

chickens scratching in chaff, old donkey
banishing fog with the warmth of his breath

woman running to grab sheets off the line
before rain blots out the smell of sun

old man playing *fútbol* with a boy
back and forth down the middle of the street

if you lived here you would know these people
you would know these animals (or you would know

the loneliness of not knowing), you would know them
but you might not see them

you might not see your brother reach for an almond
in the silver tree before he rides away

you might not see the flower etched in wood
before the doors are shut and boarded

you might not see the old ones clinging to rosaries,
the faces of those too sick to climb the chancel steps

you might not see the rooster on the peak of the roof
strutting high against the gray of the sky

what we see by walking through goes with us
what we don't see in our own village is lost

until grief pulls us close, like morning calendula
so sudden and orange in the fog

      —KCJ

IV

Tandem

Don't we all want to go it alone at times

    temper our metal, silence the conversation
    and face
    the monologue within
    make the journey with nothing
    but our own wiles

    meet the uncertainty of a dark wood
    or steep terrain of sliding rocks
    open fields of thirst, with no one
    to confirm the next step or next stop

    spend moments alone
    with spirits in the murk
    bygone travelers over the self-same ruts
    whose wooden wheels pushed through mud
    their steps apace with ours

    or seize the opportunity of a sideways tack
    a nap beneath a tree
    a finger in the dust to check
    the direction of the sun?

But moving in tandem is its own miracle.

Was it accidental
you and I left the same prints,
our leather boots identical
but for size, their respective grit
sifting and merging between us?
Was it their sympathetic strides
that kept us side by side
when we drifted apart?

The path
from Villafranca Montes de Oca
dove so far into the valley
there was nowhere to go
but up. And on the other side
after a climb
when we looked back from the top
a pair of shadows followed in our tracks
people (ahead of more)
who know by name
this fellowship that allows us
in a dizzying moment
to be alone together.

        -RR

All the Marys

dream in Navarrete, September 15, 2019

All the Marys I have ever known
(and some as yet unknown) are gathered
in an old stone hall. They keep coming through
the door, and one Mary, excited so many showed up
to help, buzzes around with towels and linens piled high
in her arms. Another Mary is tired and lies down quietly on
the cold cobblestone floor, cradling her head in her hands. She
has no blanket and doesn't ask for one, but she asks me to bring
her a cup of warm cider. Something in the way she asks makes
me want to find it right away, and I set off. I get distracted
stopping to do things, forgetting where to find supplies
but finally, I pour the cider in a white chipped cup
and walk fast down the corridor, trying to get
back to the Mary I left lying on the floor.
I wake before I reach her, before I see
the joy in her face as she takes
the cup from my hand.

The next day, in Ventosa, the beer we drink
after walking all day on a rutted road
tastes *for all the world*
like honeyed cider.

—KCJ

Tended by Bells

close to the prayers of monks
close to the bells of first day

tall twiggy nests perch high on twin sides
of the stacked stone belfry in Belorado

home to storks hatched under the wing
of the gong, fledged in the shadow

of sound, note after note
falling from the edge of a huge brass bell

marking the end of a war
the birth of a prince

the birth of a bird who one day will crack
her translucent halo to let in light brighter

than her yolk, stretching wet folds of feathers
just outside the orb of the familiar

hungry to be fed, yes, but more
hungry for the sky

and because this bird was tended by bells
and fed by towering parents

she will one day witness thousands
of bells pealing at once, town to town

world to world, and an off-key hallelujah
will rise without warning in her untried throat

—*KCJ*

Belorado

And in the way of life
always a moment missed
a picture book lost, a dream
forgotten
chased over the hills of remembrance

Enter
        a village sleepy with morning
        its overnight itinerants
        long gone, men sweeping
        the stones outside *albergues*
        and cafés, the crumbs
        of breakfasts swallowed in haste
Too late
        for morning, too early
        for evening, no beds
        for hours
Yet imagine
        the streets filled with song
        maybe dance, crowds of pilgrims
        or tourists, moonlight on murals
        bursting with scarlet and teal

        colors shine
        differently now in the mid-morning sun
        on someone's boxed magenta blooms
Pause
        in the stillness
        feel the longing
        the need to stay
        wish back time
        while the road beckons you
        toward the next town
        yearn for a slower step
        that might bring you to another village
        you will not have to pass without

Knowing

              —RR

The Olive Grove

it seems as if the grove has always been here, waiting

just past a field of hay, rough gold bales
stacked high against a darkening sky

just off the path, you will find it—
old chairs under dusty olive leaves
a huge wooden spool for a table
a young man with soft eyes who gives things away

cold water, cut tomatoes
a paper cup of wine

it might not be his grove at all

maybe he borrowed it from a farmer who knows
olives aren't enough to give to the world

maybe the farmer loves him
and lets him open the grove to passersby
because he knows the world needs trees to pause under
and water just for the asking

—continued

the young man looks too gentle for the world
but maybe the grove gives him something to stand on
because when the wine is gone, it is gone
the fruit also has its last bite
and then he can steal away to the comfort of a tent
concoct a pot of garlic soup on a tiny burner
and eat the heel of the give-away bread
he saved for dipping

we are still walking, but the moon
rises high in the east
taking its time to walk across the sky
paying no toll for its passage
through the constellations
through the olive grove
rejoicing, not just in the abundance
of the Compostela
but in the field of minor stars
lighting the way when light is scarce

like olives and grapes when least expected
in an unmarked grove just north of the path

—KCJ

What I Didn't Know

These things we take for granted
        speed, cleanliness, results

irrelevant when my only job
was to get up and walk, to move my body
through space, learn to move
without thinking about the end

People leave stones along the way
        for loved ones and for the lost

parts of themselves, too
cairns in tiny villages, turrets
rock piles shaped like hearts to mark
endings and beginnings

I brought no stones
        so gathered them instead

slipped the brown and white
and orange of Spain into my pockets
and never found a way
to leave one behind

—continued

What I didn't know then was how
        she would leave before I was ready

my sister, who always knew how
to disregard the end, celebrate
each step, not just return each smile
but provoke it

What I didn't know was how
        I had taken the loved and the lost

back home with me, held them
close until they grew substance

no longer stones but whispers
of comfort when she slipped away

        —RR

V

Laundry on the Camino

too tired to talk, we wash our clothes
in cold water and hang them in scarce space
on the line, turquoise shorts
next to the plaid shirt of a stranger
a man who speaks another language
a woman who smiles in mine

a mosaic of chance

we let go the fog, the dust, the sweat
of today, we shed it all in a basin of water

the ache of the last five miles
the doubt of the last five years
the angst of finding a bed
the fragile hope of sleep

tomorrow we will reach for our boots
daring to walk west again
but tonight
we sit in the late day sun
close to long lines of wet wool socks
close to the ripeness of figs and almonds and olives
close to wine and paella in a pan so big
it feeds us all

peppers, tomatoes and golden herbs
swirling together like clothes on the line
like songs on a ukulele

and whether or not we sleep,
in the blind time just before dawn
we will pull on clothes that smell as sweet
as the saffron air of Spain

       —KCJ

Ablutions

Here is where we mingle
one clothespin at a time. A
scavenged one here, a borrowed
one shared with the next shirt over.
We find a way
for all our socks and towels
quick-dry pants and underthings
to fraternize, communal
and shameless. While the sun
smiles upon them
our clothes turn self-possessed
brazen and flapping

at our undress.
In the afternoon breeze, festooned
in hand-laundered garments, the lines
brush against each other, then
wanton, whip themselves
into festive and intimate dance—
the fleshless skeleton
of a Spanish church as backdrop.

We pray
our clothes will dry before sunset
skip the nighttime frolics, spare
us the further indignity
of a damp and wrinkled display come
morning.

So little do we carry
that every afternoon repeats
this cycle of wash and wear,
comrades in pilgrimage bowed
before the sink, knobs of soap
like holy objects
scrubbing away the red dirt
that blessed each step.
And in this communion
—sleeve over collar under hem—
we might hear
        a laugh on the breeze
        a conversation in the weave.

—RR

The Man in the White Linen Suit

He sat at a sidewalk café
in the sunned stone streets
of Burgos, and he was not alone

the woman with silver-streaked hair
might have been a partner, the laughing
younger ones, grown children

it was too late in the afternoon
for coffee, but the dark layered liquid
with cream floating on top

drew me to his side to ask.
"A Lolita," he said in perfect English
"you must ask the bartender.

It's not on the menu, but
if you ask, he will make it."
And he was right. The bartender

scowled away our camera
but layered sugar, Drambuie
coffee then cream

into a tall clear glass
topped with scraps
of dark chocolate

and one luscious sip later I vowed
to never walk away
from a man with an open face

dressed in white linen
surrounded by love and coffee
at five o'clock in the afternoon.

—*KCJ*

Alchemy

What he said with a twist of his head
two fingers deep in the glass
his clutch on a key-sized spoon
swirls of gold bringing me to blush
and my camera lens an affront: "No.
My recipe."

How was he to know
I wouldn't steal it, take it back with me
open my own café-bar and bistro
make my fortune from his dear sweet
Lolita?

And when the drink was drunk
and me a little too, all I wanted
was another and this time
I'd watch him,
commit each step to mind
imprison the makings
in mnemonic, sear my eyes
to the glass and the bottle
and the short-handled spoon,
steal his bartender heart
and carry it away.

Did he suspect me
a foreigner? Did he know
he held the key
to my bliss on this golden afternoon
in a corner of a plaza on a Spanish street
I will never find again?

You might say
the Drambuie or the sugar-lemon twist
the coffee and cream swell rising
above the neck of that glass or some more
mysterious ingredient
felled me.
But I think it was

the latch on his smile
the chemist in his stare
the swirl of my heart
in the lock.

—RR

Rogue in the House
of Santo Domingo

Croc of the walk
killer in the cathedral
what evil nettled
this sculptor? What eleventh-century
mania
what ecstatic dance
gave birth
to you? Hiding
in the puddle of robe
at the foot
of some humorless saint
an accidental egg
buried like emerald
        the green of crayon
        and cartoon monsters
a joke, a stealthy riddle
only the very curious
or lowly
        too abased or abused to look
        a pinioned saint in the eyes
would discover (with grins)
lifting that pious hem for a peek
at the newly hatched

      the truly miraculous
      survive centuries of unseeing

You
fallen from grace, rolled across
sacred tiles, lodged in a wrinkle
where the purely terrestrial
will detect   you
not just your teeth but
the laugh itself   ferocious
the flimflam in your eyes
steals the show   urges
us to our knees
lures us down
to a peasant's polish
on the scales
of your curling tail,
      the monstrous curve
           in the arch of your brow
                the most predatory thing
                      about you

    —RR

Unwitnessed

we have seen enough cathedrals
to expect statues and crosses and vaulted stone—
what we don't expect is a beast of the swamp
circling the feet of our tall saintly saints

alligators don't live in Spain

we can't ask the eleventh century mason
why he put a reptile in a cathedral, we can only be startled
by the rough teeth and scaley tail of a leviathan creature
who stands closer to us than we are to the face of the saint

its dank breath, its terrible red eyes
lighting up all the fears we cannot name or outrun—
what we wish we had held in our arms
but didn't
what we wish we could let go
what we left for dead by the side of the road

we cannot know it, but there will be a time we need this beast
in our bellies, this desire to open wide our own unmasked mouths
not to consume the righteous or the damned
but to taste again
every morsel of the life we had to shun when plague stalked the air
when God sheltered at home
when cathedral doors clanged shut and in the dark, unwitnessed

stone saints befriended stone alligators

even the rough scales on the fearsome tail
even the mistakes of the saints

and because we share the same air
all that nonsense about body and soul being enemies
can be finally put to rest

    —KCJ

VI

Rearview

The wrong turn was not immediately obvious.
Around every section of chain link, sure we'd see
the familiar sight of town and spire
we walked on.

And when the way became too long
too wide, soiled by the rush of steel
and abandon, cars and their outposts, parts
of town we had to admit we'd hoped not
to know about—
we turned back.

Where was the verdant babble, the river-
walk we expected, the lacework sky
the bridge, the welcoming entry point
we'd grown accustomed to?

But the way back was nowhere and the way
forward was all
there was, this grimy and downtrodden
car-lot and hotel-casino-lined thoroughfare.
Fellow pilgrims, recognizable
under turtle shells of belongings, gone
into the gray morning
we walked alone.

That I'd be relieved
to see a church! Bent as in prayer
we re-tied our bootlaces, reassessed the miles.

—continued

A much bigger city
than either of us knew.

The next day we hunted down
the river. Reclaiming the walk,
we reversed course
erased all memory of the wrong turn
and its oily sheen—
Entered the town again.

Here was the green breeze redolent
with willow and water, stones and clouds
a road we'd promised ourselves. Yet
even in this moment, how could we
unknow

the outskirts, where people
still drove to work, traversed gray
mornings. Tried not to look
in the rearview mirror.
And did they know

they had a choice? Did we?
Always
arriving somewhere
the next town, the next
conversation, stepping into the next
moment, so many points of entry, so many
paths but only one

at a time.

―RR

Entering Burgos

We got lost on the outskirts of town

intending to enter the old city first
with a pastoral stroll by the river, a wrong turn
at the barbed wire airfield had us plodding
past billboards and fences and ugly concrete

we never found the river

so tired we could not think
about going back to find the right path
we rested outside a church stuccoed in grime
(never guessing what churches lay ahead)
and you said we could have a do-over
after we were safe and sheltered
we could backtrack on the river path
and enter the city again

that thought was enough to get me to the next church
where costumed townspeople danced on the plaza
the skirts of women following their feet
brilliant red and blue swishing as they turned

and one man, a little tall, a little awkward
was made handsome by the dancing—
we watched the women teach his body
again and again, to be as tall as he was

Now in the ancient part of the city
walking on stones under backlit clouds
we pass people, fresh bread tucked under their arms
and though we don't know it yet, we are close,
just two plazas from The Cathedral, The Santa Maria

We find it the next day, unburdened
from our packs but burdened enough
to marvel at the woman in the blue dress
running up a hundred steps

she wants something

she wants to breathe the mercy
of the ages, the mercy that allowed each one of us
to walk to this place
to seek the shelter of The Mother
to light candles for present griefs
and griefs not yet lived, not even imagined

she left nothing on the steps
she took it all inside

and when I look, I see that everyone here
is here, even the dead seem close to the living

—continued

the face of a young man in stone repose
so serene we want to lay a rose
on his breast, we want to console his mother
who grieves to lose so young a son
though it must have been a very long time ago

I do not know what brought me here
what made me hoist a pack and walk with pilgrims
but it has to do with running up steps
it has to do with desire
it has to do with the possibility of re-entering
Burgos on the grassy banks of a slow-flowing river
in the company of a friend who says
let's go back and see what's there
not the majesty of El Cid on his horse
but the symmetry of a very big man and a very small man
cutting brush for the city, the way they quietly heft
what they each can carry, the way their bright green vests
light up the tasks of deep shade
here because they're here
on a day in September
when Man Dance Bread Glade
are as wondrous
as Cathedral
and as holy

—KCJ

Clouds over Burgos

Down a narrow side street
a Burger King hides
behind an *Alta Pasteleria*, tricks
the eye, mine drawn away
into the clouds
over the city of Burgos
our last stop.

Tomorrow we will find our way
to a bus shelter, ask strangers overheard
speaking English—because
it is the only language we have
in common—if this is the right spot
on a roundabout full of choices. Huddling
together in anglophone angst until
the bus arrives and one woman
speaks enough Spanish to glean
a nod from a driver unwilling
to give up the details.
But despite his denial
of a train depot with that name
we arrive there, an edifice
crying it out, and wonder if
he's never taken the measure
of his own landscape. Still
we have farther to go, hours to kill
restlessly immobile
in this sparkling empty station

—continued

built for people who hardly ride trains anymore
trains where bottled water costs five euros
and more passengers stare at their phones
than at the blistered Spanish countryside
the red roofs so familiar
to us now. We pine in silent solitude.

This is good-bye. Not only to Spain
but to the road we've measured
with our boots, the fountains of
free and flowing pilgrim water
we've splashed from our bottles, the names
of villages and wine and flowers
we'll remember long into winter.

And from half-empty train
to crowded subway, to underground ride
to airport runway, our bodies hurtling
ever faster through space, the slow road
behind us—
every cell resists, every bone cries out
for one more walk
beneath the clouds
over Burgos.

—RR

VII

Making Room

Even with both parents present, herding baby quail
is a ragged operation—the adults seem unsure

which side of the street is the safe side
and with comic indecision they settle for the west.

I'm tempted to help—they seem overwhelmed—
but I'm the danger they warned their young about

so I walk as predictably as possible to my porch
letting them scatter in the bushes behind me

the parents backtrack in a frenzy to make sure all
have cleared the street, then watch me disappear inside.

This has gone on for days. They don't know I walk
to outpace human angst, not to hunt or harm, though by now

my movements are familiar to them. I walk early, I walk late
I walk long, remembering Spain, and very old nuns

helping each other up the chancel steps. We climbed stairs
in the *albergue* next door to sleep twenty to a room on pallets

so close they were touching, so close we could hear each other
breathe. Close enough to hear someone cry out in a dream

and be comforted without ever waking. Comfort sounds
the same in twenty languages, but this cannot happen now.

Strangers cannot sleep three feet apart. Just as we were getting
close to something, the world moved farther apart. It went

the other direction, away from fields of sunflowers dying
together, away from a man and his son shelling almonds

away from the offer of home-bottled vermouth in a dusty cup.
My walks are smaller now, but quail don't know the difference.

They still scuttle in clumps, settling at dusk into barberry and
bay, making room. I imagine claiming a twig in their wing-tucked

sanctuario, being the last to arrive, late and alone
in a rainstorm, someone moving over to let me in.

    —*KCJ*

Seeds

After I planted them
I forgot where.

Fat, droopy leaves
pop up among the weeds
      most likely weeds themselves
I let them breed in my mystery garden
hoping for sunbaked blooms
failing to remember the refuge for my seeds
      if not their provenance.

So my heart flies out at her cry: "It's the calendula!"

Calendula.
      Mediterranean plant of a genus that includes the common or pot marigold.

She recognizes the broad green foliage
the minute she sees it—sprouting right where
I'd buried its curlicue seeds in early spring
strategically far from the others so I'd know them
      even if I didn't recognize them
could name them
      even without memory of their color

Golden flowers in July.

In what other life were those seeds
hidden in my *España* journal,
smuggled home in my backpack?
Their flowering brings explosions of memory, places
now beyond my reach. Just one, I think, one at a time
I take in each singular echo
as it bursts from its pod.

Did I want to walk the Camino de Santiago?
she'd asked. I hesitated, my husband staring at me,
our lives growing shorter. "Why can't you?" he said.

Now, 10 months after carrying 17 pounds over 200 miles
of ancient Spanish road
I watch my first calendula bloom, its common orange
a brilliant flashback in my hugely smaller landscape.
Orange like paella and parched rooftops,
the burst of sun-ripened figs in my mouth, the glow
of church-light in soupy dawn, towns in the distance.

My western gambel oaks
hover and protect
these flashes of Spanish light that cling
to their only chance at travel, and mine.

—continued

A half-drunk bottle of *rosado* wine carried
from pilgrim's lunch to cathedral to hostel
flames into the cinematic, springs to life
in the confines of my garden. Sanctuaries
are what we make
of places we have loved.

Walking through Santo Domingo de la Calzada,
I never foresaw a town ravaged by COVID
       and were the pilgrims to blame, they wondered
       doors bolted, windows shuttered.
Tiny, dried memories
       a small village,
       a calendula patch outside a farmhouse,
       each of those 200 miles
bloom in the masked and fenced enclosure of my spare new life.
Until they blossomed, I'd begun to forget.

The sprinklers erupt, their issue renewing in these potent husks
the remembrance of elderly nuns and wooden bunkbeds,
vespers at sundown, boots shed at the door.
      Calendae. Little calendar
weeks of eating grapes off the vine, years, centuries of tradition
       carried in a handful of seeds.

      —RR

Love Letter to a Poet

for Katherine

          If ever I am
sad

          on a bridge throwing flowers in bud
          to the tune of a ukulele's tears
          trying to name petals as they fall,
          it is your words I want
          to bring me

                                          joy

          If ever I am
hungry

          on the far side of *café-con-leche-*
          bocadillo-huevos-con-chorizo-
          tortilla-de-patata-vino-tinto,
          it is your words I want
          to offer me

                                  nourishment

              If ever I am
blind

              in shards from morning glint
              off grape must and swollen vines
              labyrinthine stones catching light,
              it is your words I want
              to lend me

                                              sight

              If ever I am
alone

              on the path, in the fog
              echoes of wooden wheels carving
              weathered ruts and ghost spray,
              it is your words I want
              to give me

                                              comfort

        —RR

The Knowing that Comes
from Walking Through

for Rebecca

we thought the vineyards would last
forever because they grew beside us as we walked

always one more row of vines
always one more trough of rich, red mud
always one more chance to taste the sweet of purple
clustered into thimbles full of sun

how can we call it Old World when every year this new thing
happens—this fullness, this tongueful of summer
this last drop of late day wakening

and because we witnessed
the sun
the mud
the rain
we, too, must ripen full and fat
then give ourselves to winter wine

and in the spring, in the cold, wet desperation of blank dirt
give ourselves again to vine and meager leaf
with no guarantee of what we ripen into—
it could be a scant year, it could be brimming

but we will take the chance, again and again
until the Old Year is the new
until the New World is the old
until we can't remember deciding
to try again for harvest
because the glimmer of the next field
pulls us through
and scores of cherished grapes
make summer of us all

              —*KCJ*

Katherine January and **Rebecca Ring** met through a local writing group over ten years ago. They have long admired each other's writing and found great joy in melding their poetry into a collaborative work.

Katherine January is a semi-retired psychologist and full-time poet who lives and farms with her family in Bountiful, Utah. Blame it on her upbringing in rural Vermont or her stints as a Park Ranger in the American West, but seeds of all kinds have followed her home for decades. Katherine's writing has appeared in *Shenandoah Valley Writers'*  *Guild Showcase, The Potomac Guardian, Sine Cera, Green Ink Poetry, Cosmic Daffodil, Farmer-ish Press*, and *Last Stanza Poetry Journal*. She was awarded Honorable Mention for the Byron Herbert Reece Award sponsored by the Georgia Poetry Society. Katherine's first volume of poetry, *The Blue Giraffe*, was published in 2010.

Born in Colorado and raised in California, **Rebecca Ring** was lured to the province of Quebec by a smooth-talking French Canadian. They married and had children, and, so as not to be outnumbered, Rebecca became a Canadian too. She and her husband now reside in Utah, where Rebecca is a full-time writer. Along with degrees  in film and education and careers in both fields in Canada and the US, she has an MFA in writing from the Vermont College of Fine Arts. She writes poetry and short stories and is at work on a novel. Her publications include *Sediments Literary-Arts Journal, 21st Century Ghost Stories*, and Flame Tree Publishing's *American Gothic Short Stories. Dreams of Passing Fire* is her first poetry collection.

Shanti Arts

Nature • Art • Spirit

Please visit us online
to browse our entire book catalog,
including poetry collections and fiction,
books on travel, nature, healing, art,
photography, and more.

Also take a look at our highly regarded art
and literary journal, *Still Point Arts Quarterly*,
which may be downloaded for free.

www.shantiarts.com

www.ingramcontent.com/pod-product-compliance
Lightning Source LLC
Chambersburg PA
CBHW042134160426
43199CB00022B/2916